Life As It Could Be

Life As It Could Be

When self-help isn't enough . . .

Jon Rashbrook & Phil Brookes

MILTON KEYNES ● COLORADO SPRINGS ● HYDERABAD

14 13 12 11 10 09 08   7 6 5 4 3 2 1

First published 2008 by Authentic Media
9 Holdom Avenue, Bletchley, Milton Keynes, Bucks, MK1 1QR, UK
1820 Jet Stream Drive, Colorado Springs, CO 80921, USA
Medchal Road, Jeedimetla Village, Secunderabad 500 055, A.P., India
www.authenticmedia.co.uk

Authentic Media is a division of IBS-STL U.K., limited by guarantee, with its
Registered Office at Kingstown Broadway, Carlisle, Cumbria, CA3 0HA.
Registered in England & Wales No. 1216232. Registered charity 270162

British Library Cataloguing in Publication Data
A catalogue record for this book is available from the British Library

ISBN-13: 978-1-86024-728-6

Pale Imitation is a partnership between Jon & Phil,
for further information please visit their website www.paleimitation.com

Cover Design by David Smart
Print Management by Adare
Printed and bound in Great Britain by Bell & Bain Ltd., Glasgow

Dedicated to our friends (past and present)
at Brookwood Community Church in Woking
and Grace Ministries International in Atlanta.

With thanks to Malcolm and Liz at Authentic.
And special thanks to Alan Rashbrook
for his continuous support and encouragement.

Contents

Introduction

Life can be exhausting!

Look around you and you will see people from all walks of life rushing about trying to hold things together as best they can. We live in a society that rewards achievement and believes that modified performance, self-help and career success will provide personal fulfilment.

Unquestioningly, we frantically go about our daily living, looking to draw life from our experiences and those around us, without ever stopping to ask ourselves if this is how we were designed to be.

Like a Rubik's Cube™, we twist and turn the combinations of our life, trying to find the solution that will result in a personal sense of completeness. But what if we were actually designed to live and draw life in an entirely different way? What if there is an amazing truth, distorted to the extent that it is almost impossible for us to see it?

Life as it Could Be is a series of sixteen short, weekly studies that explore how to draw life from relationship with God, rather than through self-effort. You will journey through an understanding of the nature and character of God, think about who he created you to be, discover your true identity in him and consider how to live life as he originally intended.

Like completing a Rubik's Cube™, we can try thousands of combinations on our own, but without an understanding of how the puzzle works, we are unlikely to find the solution.

We believe that the simplest way to live life well is to understand how God originally created us to be and thereafter to allow him to reshape our lives.

We hope this book helps you on your journey with God.

Jon & Phil

life as it
could be

Week 1

Your Concept
of God

Nothing is more important in the journey of faith than a healthy concept of God. Unless we picture our God as a generous Father, full of love, compassion and grace, whose desire is *always* for our very best, our trust and faith in him will never get very far. Furthermore, without a correct concept of God, painful life experiences like suffering, bereavement and rejection can appear to be nothing more than random punishments meted out by a tyrannical dictator.

Voltaire once famously observed that 'If God made us in his image, we have certainly returned the compliment'.[1] In the absence of a clear understanding of God's character, we have each formulated a picture in our own minds of how we imagine God might be and what he might think about us.

The Bible reveals to us that because Jesus bridged the gap between God and man, believers in Christ are able to enjoy a relationship with God and discover how to live life as he originally intended. None of us will ever know the full depth and greatness of our God. However, a resolute conviction that God is 100 per cent for us and that his love is never affected by our behaviour is clearly a good starting point.

Whilst our God remains the awesome Creator of the universe who holds life in his palm, he has also become the Father who invites us to have a relationship with him.

Without a correct concept of God, painful life experiences can appear to be nothing more than random punishments

Key message

To begin the process of thinking about what God is really like, let us look at three passages in the Bible where Jesus helps shape people's understanding of the nature and character of God.

Read about the lost son – Luke 15:11–32

'But while he was still a long way off, his father saw him and was filled with compassion for him' (v.20).

Read about the woman caught in adultery – John 8:2–11

'Woman, where are they? Has no one condemned you?'

'No one, sir,' she said.

'Then neither do I condemn you,' Jesus declared. 'Go now and leave your life of sin' (vs10–11).

Read Jesus talking to Philip – John 14:8–11

Jesus answered: 'Don't you know me, Philip, even after I have been among you such a long time? Anyone who has seen me has seen the Father' (v.9).

In the story of the lost son, Jesus presented an image of the Father (representing God) demonstrating forgiveness, acceptance and compassion towards his son who had squandered all his money on wine, women and song. Notice that there is no condemnation, accusation or anger, just relief and joy that his son has returned home to the place of restoration and relationship.

With the woman caught in adultery, Jesus demonstrated these same three qualities of forgiveness, acceptance and compassion. Much like the son in the first story, the behaviour of the woman in this story put her in a position where she might expect rebuke. However, from a place of humility, she receives the very opposite.

Finally, Jesus reminds Philip that in him we see God (in a human body).

You can get a better understanding of the nature and character of God by reading the Gospel of John's account of the life of Jesus in a modern translation of the Bible such as *The Message*.

Understanding

1 People's concept of God may vary, but the majority of us tend to have a negative or at least sceptical attitude towards him, which is why faith (the ability to trust what we cannot see – Hebrews 11:1) is often difficult for us.

2 In part, we formulate our concept of God from the influential role models and authority figures in our developing years. In particular, our own father plays a significant part in this process. If your dad was absent, harsh, passive or abandoned you, it will almost certainly shape how you think about God.

3 No two people have the same concept of God. We are unique: we all have different personalities and have experienced a range of differing influences and authority figures which have combined to form the basis of what God looks like to us.

4 If we have a negative concept of God, it is usually because our personal experiences have distorted our thinking about what God might be like.

Personal application

- During the course of this week, set aside some time to consider what your God looks like. You might like to write, draw or journal your thoughts.

- Spend fifteen minutes this week thinking about how you believe God feels about you. Does this tally with the unconditional love and acceptance of the Father in the parable of the lost son or the compassion Jesus demonstrates in the story of the woman caught in adultery?

- Having watched him growing up, do you think the father in the story of the lost son was surprised how his son spent his money? Do you believe any of your life choices have shocked God?

- God never condones sinful behaviour. However, do you see any criticism in the way Jesus interacts with the woman caught in adultery?

- Do you feel peaceful at the thought of standing in front of your God today? If not, can you identify a possible reason why not?

Do you believe any of your life choices have shocked God?

Christianity made simple

Stop	**How we perceive God, shapes our faith.**

Consider *'Neither height nor depth, nor anything else in all creation, will be able to separate us from the love of God that is in Christ Jesus our Lord'* (Romans 8:39).

Action **As situations arise during this week, constantly remind yourself that God loves you unconditionally and is there for you.**

Daily prayer for Week 1

Dear Father

I want to know you better, see you more clearly and experience you daily. As I quieten my mind, please take away any false concepts of you I may have and help me to trust you more than I trust myself.

Amen

---

[1] Voltaire (François-Marie Arouet), *Le Sottisier XXXII*

life as it
could be

Week 2

Sin – Being in
Adam

As with any story, to make sense of it you need to start at the beginning, which means returning to the book of Genesis and the account of the first man and woman to walk our earth.

In the wonderful children's book *The Lion, the Witch and the Wardrobe*, author C.S. Lewis refers to the four central characters (Peter, Edmund, Susan and Lucy) as the 'Sons of Adam' and the 'Daughters of Eve'. By using these terms, Lewis was drawing the reader's attention to the biblical truth that every man, woman and child who is alive, or has ever been alive, is a direct descendant of the first man and woman to have walked the earth.

Though our personalities may differ, our skin colour may differ and our language or dialect may differ, we have one thing in common and it is something that cannot be seen. We entered this world with a spirit dead to God, which we inherited from our parents and which they received from their parents, all the way back to Adam and Eve. So, like the children in the story, we are all sons of Adam or daughters of Eve.

Our spirit is our true identity and the part of us that communicates with God. As a consequence of Adam's original sin, each one of us has been born with a spirit which is dead towards God, and we have therefore sought to derive life from whoever and wherever we can find it. Our human sinful nature (tendency toward self-serving behaviour) should therefore be seen as a state we were born into, which we inherited at birth as a result of the actions of the first man and woman.

Our spirit is our true identity

Key message

Read about the fall of man – Genesis 2:15 – 3:24

When the woman saw that the fruit of the tree was good for food and pleasing to the eye, and also desirable for gaining wisdom, she took some and ate it. She also gave some to her husband, who was with her, and he ate it (3:6).

When Adam ate from the 'tree of the knowledge of good and evil', he experienced the spiritual death that God had warned him about. From this moment on Adam (by default) had to function out of the resources of his body and soul, independently from God.

As a consequence of Adam's choice, every human being is born with a spirit which is unable to communicate with and draw upon the resources of God. As a result, we live life meeting our needs from our own resources which we will call our 'self-life'.

The Bible describes this state of being as 'sin', which it may be helpful in some circumstances to define as '**S**elf **I**ndependent **N**eed'. In this state of being we are separated from God and, as a result, manifest self-serving behaviour.

Understanding

1 The death that Adam experienced was clearly not a physical death, as he lived until he was 930 (Genesis 5:5)! Rather, his spirit became dead towards God.

2 In the New Testament, the apostle Paul refers to every human being inheriting the same spiritual death as Adam (Romans 5:12). Think of it like this: if your grandfather had not existed, then your father could not have been born and neither could

you. With this in mind, it could be said that you are 'in' your father, 'in' your grandfather and 'in' your ancestors before them, right back to Adam. Therefore, in the same way that Adam was separated from God by spiritual death, we too are born spiritually dead towards God, that is we inherit the same spiritual DNA.

3 It is for this very reason that Jesus needed to be conceived by the Holy Spirit into the lineage of Adam, enabling him to be born with a perfect spirit that was alive to God in the same way that Adam had originally been created.

4 Sin, therefore, is not only what we do (our behaviour), but is the outworking of who we are as a result of our inherited fallen state (our condition).

5 It might be helpful to think of our inherited sin as the unseen roots of a tree, with the leaves representing our actions.

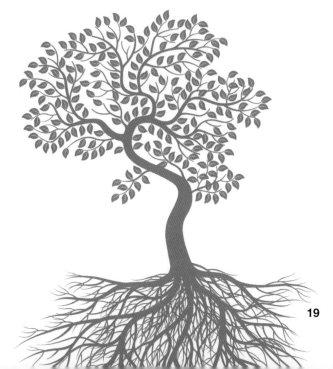

Personal application

- In the Garden of Eden Satan deceived Adam by suggesting he could become like God when, ironically, he was in fact already like God. If you have received Jesus as Lord and Saviour, you have received his righteousness and are like him in God's sight. Does this feel true to you or is Satan deceiving you as to your true identity?

- The expression 'born-again Christian', which is often used, refers to the rebirth of the spirit. When Jesus explained this concept to Nicodemus (John 3:1–8) he was showing him that the rebirth of our dead spirit, through asking God's Holy Spirit to come and live in us, allows us to enter into relationship with God. Read through this passage and consider its significance.

- In light of the above, would you agree that a human spirit is either dead or alive to God, rather than its condition being based upon good deeds, religious observance or any other human behaviour?

- Jesus was immaculately conceived of the Holy Spirit by a virgin, effectively creating a new lineage. During the course of this week, ponder whether you are 'in Adam' or 'in Christ'?

- Once we are 'in Christ' we begin the process of learning to live as God originally intended, replacing our independence with dependency on the Father. Are you still depending on yourself or growing in dependence upon God?

- During the course of this week continue to read through Genesis 2 – 3 and John 3, comparing these accounts and asking God to further illuminate our problem and his solution.

Christianity made simple

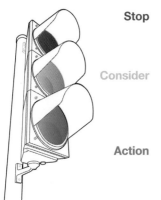

Stop **Sinfulness is the state we are born in, with sinful behaviour the product.**

Consider *'Therefore, if anyone is in Christ, he is a new creation; the old has gone, the new has come!'* (2 Corinthians 5:17)

Action **During the course of this week, spend time talking to God, knowing that he has saved you from your sin, and allow him to shape your future behaviour.**

Daily prayer for Week 2

Dear Father

Thank you that you really desire a relationship with me. Thank you that Jesus has made this possible. I am a 'new creation'; I am 'in Christ'. Please help me to remember that because of Jesus, my sin, past, present and future has been covered.

Shape my choices and behaviour in light of these truths. May it lead to greater peace and freedom.

Amen[1]

---

[1] As you pray, consider that at one time you were a sinner 'in Adam'. Now, if you have been 'born again', you are a righteous person 'in Christ', but you still retain the capacity for sinful behaviour.

life as it
could be

Week 3
Jesus and Salvation

Some people struggle with the concept of a loving heavenly Father sending his son to die a painful and unjust death. It is therefore helpful to remember what Jesus himself said to Philip (see John 14:8–11, Week 1), when he reminded him that he (Jesus) and the Father are one. This is explained at the beginning of John's gospel:

In the beginning was the Word [Jesus]*, and the Word was with God and the Word was God . . . The Word became flesh and made his dwelling among us . . . grace and truth came through Jesus Christ. No one has ever seen God, but God the One and Only* [Jesus]*, who is at the Father's side, has made him known* (John 1:1–18).

The simple truth is that God is love and perfection and, like oil and water, he and sin can never mix. Therefore, in our natural sinful state, we cannot have a relationship with God. With this in mind God, in the person of the sinless Jesus Christ, died instead of us on the cross to remove our sin and re-establish the opportunity for the relationship which had been shattered by Adam's decision to disobey him.

Jesus therefore provides each person with the opportunity to reconnect with God the Father. If we will recognize that we have sinned, recognize who Jesus is and what he accomplished by dying on the cross, and ask for forgiveness, he is able to bring to life our old, dead spirit, making it alive to the resources of God.

We are then saved from our own independent self-life and the consequences of our sin. As a result we are free to choose a relationship with God, as he always intended.

Sadly, some people have the idea that a relationship with God will subtract from their life, whereas the reality is that there are actually many additions.

Key message

Read John 3:16–17

For God so loved the world that he gave his one and only Son, that whoever believes in him shall not perish but have eternal life (v.16).

The consequence of Adam's choice in the Garden of Eden was spiritual death, both for him and his descendants. This resulted in separation from the presence of God, both in the present and in the life hereafter.

God's solution to this human state of being was to take upon himself the consequences of our sin through Jesus' sacrificial death on the cross, and ultimate resurrection. By doing this, Jesus opened up a doorway of opportunity for us to re-establish relationship with the Father here on earth and for eternity with him in heaven.

The foundation of the Christian faith is not tied up with our performance but is based on our identity. Are we in Adam or are we in Christ (Ephesians 2:8–10)?

Jesus opened up a doorway of opportunity for us to re-establish relationship with the Father

Understanding

1 Sinless perfection is the only way to enter the Kingdom of Heaven. This can either be achieved by living a sinless life, which is impossible (Romans 3:23), or by spiritual rebirth through Christ (John 3).

2 Our inherited sin prevents us from experiencing friendship with God. When we say sorry for our sin and ask Jesus to be our Saviour, we are reborn spiritually. At this moment we are freed from the hold that sin had over us (Romans 6:6–7).

3 Jesus was the only human being to have lived a sinless life, which would have enabled him to enter the Kingdom of Heaven on his own merit. Instead, he chose to die in our place, knowing that this would give us free access to God. This is the meaning of 'grace' – that Christ freely did for us what we were unable to do for ourselves.

4 The resurrection of Jesus from the dead acknowledges that death and the power of sin have been overcome. Satan believed that if he killed Jesus it would have the same devastating effect as with Adam. What he did not know was that death could not hold a blameless sacrifice, and Satan's power was defeated once and for all.

5 Salvation is the forgiveness of sin, spiritual rebirth, adoption into the lineage of Christ, empowerment by the Holy Spirit coming to live in us and the inheritance of eternal life instead of death.

Personal application

- Has there ever been a point at which you have asked Jesus to be your Saviour and received forgiveness for your sin? If not, then consider the reasons why not.

- Do you feel that you have an understanding of where sin came from and God's solution for mankind? Would you feel confident explaining these concepts to someone else?

- This week, remind yourself that, because of Jesus, your sin is forgiven and removed from God's sight and memory, *'as far as the east is from the west, so far has he removed our transgressions from us'* (Psalm 103:12).

- Have you ever encountered people who believe that personal relationship with Jesus is about cost rather than gain? What would you say to them?

- During the course of this week, think about how you would respond to a friend who wanted to know what having a relationship with God was like and how they could have one.

Do you feel that you have
an understanding of
where sin came from?

Christianity made simple

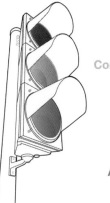

Stop **Jesus has restored the opportunity for relationship between God and man.**

Consider *'I tell you the truth, whoever hears my word and believes him who sent me, has eternal life and will not be condemned; he has crossed over from death to life'* (John 5:24).

Action **At the beginning of every day this week, take a moment to thank God that your salvation is complete in Jesus.**

Daily prayer for Week 3

Dear Father

I recognize that your desire is to have a relationship with me. I understand that, having been born into sin, I need a Saviour and that you, Jesus, are my Saviour.

Amen

---

life as it
could be

Week 4
Grace and Law

The grace of God is not easy for us to understand.

Before Jesus came to earth and died on the cross to eradicate our sins, the only way for man to attempt to live up to God's standard of perfection was to obey a strict set of rules and regulations – 'the Law'. We still have a form of the Law in society today, as a set of standards to live up to, to show right from wrong – with consequences for disobedience.

With the Law, we are either guilty or innocent, but with God there is a different way. If we humble ourselves and turn to God, we will receive what we do not deserve, namely forgiveness and acceptance. This is grace – God's undeserved favour to us.

The Bible is packed full of stories of men and women who fell short of the Law but who, through repentance, discovered the grace of God and in the process changed their future direction. Saul the Pharisee, upholder of the Law, who persecuted Christians, became Paul the apostle, the main teacher of God's acceptance through grace; Zacchaeus changed from fraudulent tax collector to a man of honesty and integrity; and, right at the end of his life, the thief on the cross next to Jesus asked for forgiveness and received grace and acceptance, and a place in heaven for eternity.

Human nature tends to reject those who fail or fall short of the standard of acceptability. With God this is not the case. He will never reject us and is always waiting to welcome us.

Human nature tends to reject those who fail or fall short of the standard of acceptability

Key message

Read Ephesians 2:1–10

For it is by grace that you have been saved, through faith – and this is not from yourselves, it is the gift of God – not by works so that no one can boast (vs 8–9).

There are two ways to God the Father: the first through perfect observance of the law, which is unachievable for us; the second through gaining the free gift of Christ's righteousness by accepting him as our Saviour.

Jesus understood that it was not that the Law was wrong, but simply that we are unable to measure up to it. As every person lives an imperfect life, this avenue of access to God through performance is closed. Therefore Jesus fulfilled the requirements of the Law by living a perfect (sinless) life, dying in our place and giving us his righteousness as a free gift of grace to those who accept it.

So none of us can boast or rely on our religious actions or behaviour because they always fall short of the mark. But through grace we are free to pursue a relationship with God and to be restored to the status he originally intended, as part of his family.

Through grace we are free to pursue a relationship with God

Understanding

1 Many Christians apply the same approach to their spiritual relationship with God as they have done in their relationships with other people, e.g. moving from people-pleasing to God-pleasing to earn acceptance. This practice can lead to religious performance, rather than a trusting relationship, which then results in pious legalism and/or spiritual fatigue.

2 The irony of this human interpretation of the gospel message is that it is in direct contradiction to the gift of grace, which is based on our identity in Christ rather than on honing our performance.

3 Many of Jesus' harshest words and greatest challenges were directed at the Pharisees for their lack of faith and desire to attain righteousness through upholding the Law. This resulted in their judgemental attitudes and their measuring people's acceptability based on their works, which contrasted with Jesus' core teaching that salvation comes through faith alone.

4 Given the fact that it is by grace that we are saved, does this give us carte blanche to do whatever we want? The apostle Paul says, *'What shall we say, then? Shall we go on sinning, so that grace may increase? By no means! We died to sin; how can we live in it any longer?'* (Romans 6:1–2) because he truly understood that to continue living in sin is in direct conflict with life and freedom in Christ.

5 God desires that we live in a grace-based relationship with him rather than one of religious obligation, moving from 'should', 'ought' and 'have to' to a life of 'peace', 'contentment' and 'freedom', with an underlying heart attitude that says, 'I desire to'.

Personal application

- During the course of this week, consider whether your relationship with God is based on the things you do or your identity in Christ.

- Do you ever find yourself thinking, 'The better I behave, the more acceptable I am to God'?

- Is your relationship with God based on law or grace? A good litmus test is whether being a Christian feels like a burden or a blessing!

- When you pray, read the Bible or go to church, is it out of obligation or desire?

- Once we understand that our relationship with God is based on grace, which is freely given and unmerited, it can result in tremendous freedom. During the next seven days, take time to thank God for his gift of grace. You may even like to write some of your thoughts down.

Is your relationship with God
based on law or grace?

Christianity made simple

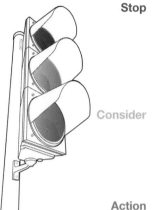

Stop Religious observance scores no points with God. Only through receiving Christ's righteousness, which is freely given, can we be reconciled to him.

Consider *'I do not set aside the grace of God, for if righteousness could be gained through the law, Christ died for nothing!'* (Galatians 2:21)

Action This week try and find the words to the hymn 'Amazing Grace' by John Newton from the Internet or in a hymn book. Read through them and meditate on God's wonderful gift to you.

Daily prayer for Week 4

Dear Father

Thank you so much that there is nothing I can do to earn your love or acceptance. It is so wonderful to be free to enter into relationship with you because of what Jesus has done for me.

Help me to replace the lies that I have believed about myself and you, with the truth of who you are, your grace, your love and your mercy.

Amen

life as it
could be

Week 5
**The Blueprint of
Humanity**

Many people who believe in a spiritual realm think of themselves as a physical being with a spirit somewhere inside them. The Bible, however, declares that human beings are made in the image of God (Genesis 1:26) – and God is not constrained by a human body, he is Spirit. We then, being made in his image, are spiritual beings with an earthly body, rather than the other way around.

This understanding not only helps us to better grasp the need for a concept of spiritual rebirth, it also enables us to better understand the deterioration of our physical bodies within the context of our true identity.

The apostle Paul refers to the make-up of man as being spirit, soul and body (1 Thessalonians 5:23). This differential is particularly helpful in understanding why our spirit is either dead or alive to God, whilst our soul (our personality) is the part of us that is in a continual process of transformation.

It may be helpful to consider that when our spirit becomes alive to God, it acts like a spring of fresh water which flows into our soul (our mind, emotions and will), influencing our desires and subsequent behaviour.

We, being made in his image, are spiritual beings with an earthly body

Key message

A clear understanding of God's blueprint for humanity is really helpful when looking to establish relationship with him. Simply put, we are tripartite (three-part) beings, made up of spirit, soul and body.

Read 1 Thessalonians 5:23

May God himself, the God of peace, sanctify you through and through. May your whole spirit, soul and body be kept blameless at the coming of our Lord Jesus Christ.

Our spirit is the part of us that relates to God, which is dead from birth and is given new life through faith in Christ.

Our soul is how we relate to other people and comprises our mind, our will and our emotions.

Our body is our dwelling place, from which our speech, our actions and five senses derive.

Many Christians experience a conflict between their spiritual perfection in Christ and their tendency towards sinful behaviour. Armed with a better knowledge of how we were created, we really can grow in faith, through an understanding of our fallen state at birth, our rebirth into relationship with God and our transformation thereafter. You could think of this process as realigning yourself spiritually with God, or spiritual realignment.

Understanding

1 Every human being is born with a spirit dead to God. This spirit, however, though dead to God is alive to 'self', the values of our fallen world and the deceptions of Satan, the enemy of God and man.

2 Our soul really is the battleground where our renewed spirit clashes with our learnt forms of self-survival. Within this realm, our mind begins to be renewed by learning to accept ourselves as God sees us, rather than on the basis of our previous history or our current performance. It is in the area of our soul that we learn to overcome our default behaviour and stand against the seduction of what society says will bring fulfilment.

3 Once our spirit becomes alive to God through faith in Jesus (born again), our bodies become home to the living presence of God's Spirit – the Holy Spirit. Paul referred to this by calling our body the 'temple of the Holy Spirit' (1 Corinthians 6:19). With this in mind, we should take care of our physical bodies, whilst not falling into the temptation of trying to find our identity or self-worth in our outward appearance.

4 Once we are born again, we enter a process of learning to filter out the distractions of the world in order to hear God's voice and learn to live life his way, rather than our own established way of living. The reason we do this is not out of a sense of duty but to genuinely experience something far more life-giving, personally rewarding and honouring to God. With this change in focus, we start an exciting lifelong journey of spiritual formation.

Personal application

- This week, think about how it is possible for you to be perfect in God's sight, yet still be capable of sinful behaviour.

- Is your peace and security derived from how you feel about yourself and the opinions of others or from the truth of God's love and purpose for you?

- Consider how much of your personal well-being is wrapped up in your physical appearance.

- During the week think about what you expose yourself to. Can you think of anything or anyone that could cause conflict in your soul?

- Do you believe that your spirit coming alive to God adds to or subtracts from the uniqueness of your personality?

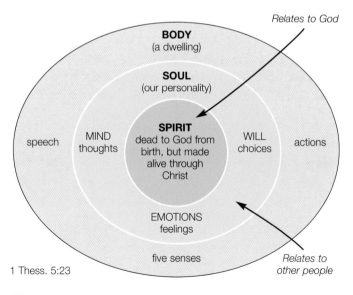

1 Thess. 5:23

Christianity made simple

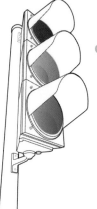

Stop **God created us as spiritual beings, with a body and a soul.**

Consider *'So God created man in his own image, in the image of God he created him; male and female he created them'* (Genesis 1:27).

Action **This week, consider God's blueprint for humanity and your life. Ask him to help you live life from your spiritual centre rather than draw from the resources of your body and soul.**

Daily prayer for Week 5

Dear Father

Help me to surrender my body to my soul, my soul to my spirit and my spirit to you. I am learning that living life out of my own resources is not the best way.

Help me to learn how to draw life from your Holy Spirit through my spirit. May it lead to the abundant life that Jesus spoke of.

Amen

life as it
could be

Week 6
The Flesh

As we have already seen, God's original blueprint for humanity was to live life in relational dependence upon him, in an environment where our identity, self-worth and needs would be fully met by him. However, when our spirit died to God, the intended focus of our worship died too and was replaced with a form of coping based upon independence and a preoccupation with ourselves.

Paul refers to this form of coping as our 'flesh', which is diametrically opposed to living life from the spirit and drawing on God's resources and provision for our needs.

Reference to 'the flesh', 'in the flesh' or 'fleshly' appears in seven of the New Testament letters (Romans 7, 8 & 13; 1 Corinthians 5; Galatians 5, Ephesians 2; Philippians 3; Colossians 2; 2 Peter 2). It is a subject that many Christians know little about, and yet is fundamental to understanding why we behave as we do. One of the most popular versions of the Bible, *The New International Version*, translates the Greek words *sarx, sarkikos* and *sarkos* as 'sinful nature' rather than the word 'flesh', but for the purposes of understanding here 'flesh' is more helpful.

Our flesh, therefore, in this context does not relate to our physical bodies, nor is it limited to hedonistic desire. Instead the word is used to describe a believer's old way of coping with life prior to being born again and reconnecting to the resources of God. The subsequent daily battle in the life of a Christian is to choose to draw on God from our renewed spirit, rather than fall back on our all too familiar default patterns of coping in our own strength out of our body and soul.

Key message

Read Galatians 5:13–26 (NASB¹) and Romans 7:14–25

For you were called to freedom, brethren; only do not turn your freedom into an opportunity for the flesh, but through love serve one another. For the whole Law is fulfilled in one word, in the statement, 'YOU SHALL LOVE YOUR NEIGHBOR AS YOURSELF.' But if you bite and devour one another, take care that you are not consumed by one another. But I say, walk by the Spirit, and you will not carry out the desire of the flesh. For the flesh sets its desire against the Spirit, and the Spirit against the flesh; for these are in opposition to one another, so that you may not do the things that you please. But if you are led by the Spirit, you are not under the Law (Galatians 5:13–18, NASB).

The whole subject of the flesh is quite a difficult concept for us to grasp. However, the more we understand both our own behaviour and the behaviour of others in the context of this inherited form of coping, the more we are able to grow in awareness of the battle for pre-eminence between our true identity in Christ and our old false identity in self.

The flesh, as Paul refers to it, is the way we, as fallen human beings, have formed coping mechanisms in order to live life in our own strength. Everyone has unique flesh, shaped by their own experiences and beliefs about themselves.

Recognition of what flesh is and what our individual flesh looks like, is fundamental in the process of experiencing life in Christ, although the familiar nature of our flesh makes it difficult for us to distinguish between 'flesh life' and 'spiritual life'.

Our flesh does not disappear when we become Christians, instead we engage in a daily battle to overcome our default self-reliance in order to gain an eternal perspective.

Understanding

1 The concept of our flesh is not an easy thing to get our minds around. It is our mental and physical coping: the place from where we draw our identity and self-worth outside of our relationship with God. Try picturing it as a suit of armour which we construct through life in order to protect and equip, and which has 'It's all about me!' written across the breastplate.

2 Galatians 5:17 says that the flesh and the Spirit are in total opposition to each other. God never designed us to cope independently, but to live abundantly in relationship with him. We can choose either to draw from him or from our own personal resources but never both at the same time.

3 The process of spiritual growth involves a tug of war between our flesh and our renewed spirit. Paul says in Romans 7:18–19: *'For I have the desire to do what is good, but I cannot carry it out. For what I do is not the good I want to do; no, the evil I do not want to do – this I keep on doing.'* It takes a conscious decision to respond out of our spirit.

4 In order to illustrate the difference, in Galatians 5:19–26 Paul lists examples of what living life out of the flesh and living life out of the spirit actually look like. *'The acts of the sinful nature* [flesh] *are obvious: sexual immorality, impurity and debauchery; idolatry and witchcraft; hatred, discord, jealousy, fits of rage, selfish ambition . . . But the fruit of the Spirit is love, joy, peace, patience, kindness, goodness, faithfulness, gentleness and self-control . . .'*

5 Inevitably our flesh will, at some point or another, prove to be inadequate for living life. It is at these crunch points in life that we often experience 'meltdown' or 'brokenness' (see Week 14), because we have literally come to the end of ourselves. We have exhausted the resources of our independence and are now in a position to experience a different way of living. Simply put, death to self allows room for life in Christ.

6 The enemy always wants to steer us back to flesh-based behaviour, because life lived in our own strength will always prevent us from experiencing Christ's provision of spiritual life.

Personal application

- In living the Christian life, can you relate to what Paul is talking about in Romans 7:15–25? That is, do you find yourself engaging in behaviour or activities which you know to be contrary to what you really want to do?

- In order to be able to engage with Christ, we need to be able to disengage with our flesh. In order to be able to do this, we need to gain a better understanding of what our flesh looks like.

- The apostle Paul recognized that he had performance-based, religious flesh, which he understood to be worthless. He also recognized that salvation, life and freedom can only be found in Christ (Philippians 3:1–11). This week consider how your flesh is structured – how you cope with your personal fears in the context of daily living. You might rely on physical intimidation, your knowledge, humour, boasting, people-pleasing, financial security, etc.

- Finally, consider whether your prayers revolve around your personal desires (self) or God's purposes for your life.

Christianity made simple

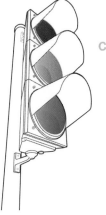

Stop **Flesh and Spirit are in opposition to each other!**

Consider *'But I say, walk by the Spirit, and you will not carry out the desire of the flesh. For the flesh sets its desire against the Spirit, and the Spirit against the flesh; for these are in opposition to one another, so that you may not do the things that you please'* (Galatians 5:16–17 NASB).

Action **You have a choice – to operate out of flesh or to invite the Lord to show you how to live out of his Spirit, according to his will.**

Do you find yourself engaging in behaviour or activities which you know to be contrary to what you really want to do?

Daily prayer for Week 6

Dear Father

I am so familiar with the way I cope with life that I find it difficult to look beyond this to the possibility that things could be different.

This week reveal to me what my own flesh looks like and enable me to experience more of your provision as I go about my daily life.

Thank you that, because of Jesus, you love me regardless of my flesh and that your desire for me is to experience total freedom and life in abundance.

Amen

---

[1] The *New American Standard* version of the Bible (NASB) lends itself to an accurate translation of what Paul is communicating regarding the flesh, while *The Message* translation communicates this difficult teaching in a simple, easily readable way.

life as it
could be

Week 7

The Believer's
Identity

What is True of Christ is True of You

Who am I? Ever since the perfect bond of unity between God and man was broken in the Garden of Eden, every one of us has sought to identify and associate with something or someone who will fill the void.

This deep-rooted need to belong and feel valued drives each individual to pursue self-acceptance through association.

Our identity is derived from what or who we choose to associate ourselves with, whether it is our job, the car we drive, where we live, or even the football team we support. However, often these substitute identities can leave us discontented, striving for more, or living in fear of losing what we have.

One of the greatest gifts resulting from being in the family of God is that we exchange our old identity for a new one in Christ. That which is true of Christ is now true of you because you are 'in Christ' and have become part of his family.

Substitute identities can leave us discontented, striving for more, or living in fear of losing what we have

Key message

Read Galatians 2:20

I have been crucified with Christ and I no longer live, but Christ lives in me. The life I live in the body, I live by faith in the Son of God, who loved me and gave himself for me.

This passage encapsulates the exchange of identity that occurs when you become a Christian. At the moment you ask Jesus to be your Saviour, God lifts you 'out of Adam' and places you 'into Christ'. In other words, you actually exchange your old identity in Adam for your new identity in Christ.

In God's eyes you are Christ-like in your new identity, even though you may not feel it or behave like it to begin with. As you grow in your new identity, the things you used to associate yourself with will tend to become less significant.

Understanding

1 One of the first things Adam realized after his rebellion in the Garden of Eden was that he was naked and felt exposed and vulnerable. When we don't know who we are, we tend to cover our vulnerability with false identity.

2 Have you ever noticed that when you are introduced to someone new, the question that often follows is 'What do you do?' Typically, we define our personal identity through what we do, how well we do it and what others think of us.

3 One of the dangers of creating our identity through chosen associations is that we construct an identity 'mask' which we present to the world and hide behind. Although this mask can serve us well, it often prevents us from living open and transparent lives.

4 God's provision, through Christ, enables us to be set free from this false identity driven by self-need, and instead find our security, value and self-worth through our relationship with him.

5 After becoming a Christian, the temptation is to continue living out of 'self' (walking in the flesh), i.e. continuing to live the way we always have rather than living in light of our new identity (walking in the Spirit).

When we don't know who we are, we tend to cover our vulnerability with false identity

Personal application

- Everyone desires to feel special, important, respected and recognized. Over the next seven days, think about your life and identify the associations and choices you have made to meet these needs. Make a list of them so that they become familiar to you.

- Consider whether you believe a deepening relationship with the Lord can begin to replace dependency on some of these associations.

- Remember that God's desire is always for our very best. He never wants to take good things from us, but rather to replace our artificial securities with the real thing. Are there any associations on your list that you genuinely fear losing?

- Ideally, find a quiet place this week, free from interruption, and ask the Lord what your new identity in Jesus looks like. Write down any words, names or pictures that he gives you.

- We were created for relationship with God. Everything we do should flow from this central focus. For example, a Christian doctor is a son of God who practises medicine, rather than a medical professional who also goes to church. It is a question of priority, which Jesus addresses in Matthew 6:33: *'But seek first his kingdom and his righteousness, and all these things will be given to you as well.'* Consider this passage in the context of your own daily living.

- Our lives are like having a handful of rough-cut stones, some diamonds and some glass. We are unable to see the difference, but the Lord examines them for us and, if we are willing, will sort them for us, discarding the glass and leaving the diamonds. It is our personal experience that as we have opened our clenched fists to this process (which has required considerable faith), the Lord's adequacy has surpassed our expectations.

Christianity made simple

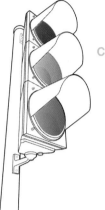

Stop   **What is true of Christ is true of you.**

Consider   *'I have been crucified with Christ and I no longer live, but Christ lives in me. The life I live in the body, I live by faith in the Son of God, who loved me and gave himself for me'* (Galatians 2:20).

Action   **Think about the exchange that has taken place between your old identity and your new identity in Christ. If you are able, watch Walt Disney's *The Lion King* as this beautifully illustrates the danger of allowing fear to rob us of our true identity.**

Daily prayer for Week 7

Dear Father

I recognize that in my new identity I am a new creation, a child of God, Christ's friend. I thank you that I can express Christ's life because he is my life.

I thank you that in your eyes I am righteous and holy. Please enable me to understand fully who I am in you and who you created me to be.

Amen

life as it
could be

Week 8

Jesus and Spiritual Maturity

When our spirit has been 'born again' or made alive 'in Christ' we are able to begin a new way of living life. This is what the apostle Paul was referring to when he wrote his second letter to the Church in Corinth: *'Therefore, if anyone is in Christ, he is a new creation; the old has gone, the new has come!'* (2 Corinthians 5:17).

However, new believers need to be aware that the journey towards maturity in Christ does not happen overnight. Our past is taken care of by the single decision to ask Jesus to be our Lord and Saviour; spiritual maturity, by contrast, occurs by making the decision to choose to draw on Christ's strength day by day, moment by moment.

When we are united with God through Christ we are made perfect in his sight forever. However, our familiarity with drawing on our own strength, rather than accessing the resources of Christ, is an ongoing battle in the life of a believer.

Spiritual maturity occurs as we allow the love of Christ and his values to reshape us and strengthen us as we learn to overcome the temptations and values of this world, our own flesh and the whispering deception of Satan.

Simply put, there is no substitute for spending time with the Lord, learning to hear his voice and becoming sensitive to his leading.

The journey towards maturity in Christ does not happen overnight

Key message

Read Matthew 11:28–29

'Come to me, all you who are weary and burdened, and I will give you rest. Take my yoke upon you and learn from me, for I am gentle and humble in heart, and you will find rest for your souls.'

Having committed our lives to Jesus, there is a tendency for many of us to view our salvation as simply an eternal insurance policy for when we die. This attitude of mind, which eliminates God from our day to day living, can produce self-serving behaviour which robs us of experiencing God's best for our lives. Another mistake is to continually look to earn God's acceptance through our religious performance, which can lead to legalistic and judgemental behaviour.

Jesus provides the perfect example for us of how to live the Christian life. We ask Jesus to be our Saviour just once, but we need to ask him to be our guide and sufficiency every day, not out of obligation, but out of a desire to attain more of the peace and freedom that he spoke of throughout his earthly ministry.

Similarly, the apostle Paul sets out guidelines in his letter to the Romans (particularly chapters 5 – 8), to help us in the process of achieving a realignment from self to Christ.

Understanding

1 From the outset, it is important to understand and experience the truth that the apostle Paul communicates in his letter to the Ephesians, which is that it is by grace that we are saved, not by anything we can do, in and of ourselves (Ephesians 2:8).

2 Through understanding this truth, we can begin to walk in the freedom that Jesus promised, which is developed in an ongoing process of spiritual maturity.

3 God's ultimate desire is for relationship with you, and disciplines such as prayer, reading the Bible and meeting with other believers can really deepen this process. However, it is important not to put yourself under strict rules (law) as this can often detract from the enjoyment and freedom of intimate relationship with God.

4 It is from this place of freedom that the 'Good News' really feels like good news! And the 'exchanged life' (i.e. exchanging life 'in Adam' for life 'in Christ') can really begin to feel like liberation.

5 'Ministry' is not an activity or an obligation. Rather it is the practical outworking of the life of Christ within us, as he helps others through us.

Personal application

- Have you ever considered that it is all about what God has done for you and nothing to do with what you can do for him?

- During the course of this week, read through Ephesians 2:8–10 and consider what the 'grace of God' actually means to you.

- Does your relationship with the Lord go beyond having secured your eternal salvation?

- Jesus had a wonderful living relationship with God the Father. Make a list of the priorities and lifestyle choices which you think enabled this to happen.

- Do you think these priorities are relevant for your life and do you think it is possible for you to experience something similar?

- Have you ever thought of God as a loving Father and considered that, like any loving parent, he desires the best for you. Have you experienced this truth for yourself?

Does your relationship with the Lord go beyond having secured your eternal salvation?

Christianity made simple

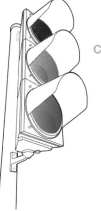

Stop   **Jesus' priority was always his relationship with the Father.**

Consider   *'Jesus gave them this answer: "I tell you the truth, the Son can do nothing by himself; he can do only what he sees his Father doing, because whatever the Father does the Son also does"'* (John 5:19).

Action   **This week, try talking to the Lord, as you would to a close friend, in everything you do – work, rest and play.**

Daily prayer for Week 8

Jesus

I recognize that your relationship with the Father was one of love, trust and intimacy. I understand that because of what you achieved on the cross, I am a child of God.

As I develop in my own relationship with the Father, help me to hear his voice and walk according to his will.

Amen

life as it
could be
Week 9
Forgiveness

Forgiveness is both the most wonderful gift to receive, and appears to be one of the most costly to give!

For a Christian, knowing that we are forgiven by God and will always be acceptable to him is the most liberating and freeing discovery. For those of us who have carried a sense of guilt, shame or regret for past choices or actions, receiving God's forgiveness can feel like being washed clean from the grime of our past.

Whilst receiving forgiveness is a liberating experience, extending it to others can feel like a different story. The pain of being wronged by another person can touch the inner core of our being and, emotionally, we are more inclined to want to consider revenge than forgiveness. The greatest tragedy, however, is that when we refuse to forgive, the bitterness, anger and hurt is never satisfied. If left unchecked, lack of forgiveness can sour our whole outlook, affecting not only our relationships, but our own emotional and mental health.

Ultimately, unforgiveness acts as the greatest barrier to us experiencing the freedom of Christ in our own lives. It is for this reason that, when teaching the people to pray, Jesus said *'Forgive us our sins, for we also forgive everyone who sins against us'* (Luke 11:4).

Whilst receiving forgiveness is a liberating experience, extending it to others can feel like a different story

Key message

Read Matthew 26:28

'This is my blood of the covenant, which is poured out for many for the forgiveness of sins.'

Forgiveness is a two-fold process of giving and receiving through understanding: firstly, that our debt (a result of our sin) to God has been paid through Christ's blood and, secondly, that in order to walk in the freedom Jesus promised, we need to learn to forgive others in the same way we have been forgiven.

Understanding

1 Often our attitude towards forgiveness can lead us to believe that when extended to others, we are 'letting them off the hook' for the pain they have caused us. In truth, forgiveness is actually the cancelling of a debt in order that we ourselves can walk free. In practice, ask yourself who is affected more through an attitude of unforgiveness, you or the other person?

2 It is impossible to have intimate relationship with another person whilst a state of unforgiveness exists between the two parties. It is equally impossible for us to experience meaningful relationship with the Lord if a state of unforgiveness exists. It is for this very reason that our sins (past, present and future) were removed from the equation at the cross.

3 Have you considered that at the point of your salvation, Christ's forgiveness covered all your past and future sins, because when Jesus died and rose again about 2,000 years ago, you had not been born, and *all* your sins were in the future!

4 In Christ we are totally forgiven and in God's sight righteous. However, we still make choices that are not consistent with our new status. Therefore, as part of the ongoing process towards spiritual maturity, we need to acknowledge our sinful behaviour, tell God we are sorry and thank him for his forgiveness.

5 It is important to understand that post-salvation we enter into a state of total forgiveness from God's perspective, i.e. God always sees us as righteous – our slate completely wiped clean. With this in mind, the purpose of asking God's forgiveness is all about our freedom rather than God's acceptance.

6 Based on a true understanding of God's forgiveness, we are able to live life in total freedom, using our failures to shape our character into Christ's image (which is grace), rather than as instruments of chastisement (which is law).

Is there anything in your life that you believe God is unable to forgive you for, or that you are unwilling to forgive yourself for?

Personal application

- Does your prayer life involve an endless cycle of 'Father forgive me for . . .' If so, how does this impact on your relationship with God? Do you feel you are currently experiencing unconditional and eternal forgiveness?

- Which of the following statements do you believe to be most true?

    – A Christian is someone whose sins have been completely forgiven.

    – A Christian is someone who spends their life doing 'good deeds' in order to earn God's forgiveness.

- Consider how each of these statements could impact upon the depth and nature of your relationship with God.

- During the course of this week, make a list of anyone from whom you are withholding forgiveness. Think through the effect this has on you, your relationship with the other person and ultimately your relationship with God.

- Is there anything in your life that you believe God is unable to forgive you for, or that you are unwilling to forgive yourself for? If so, add these to your list.

- Do you fully understand that God's forgiveness is rooted in your identity in Jesus rather than your daily choices and behaviour?

Christianity made simple

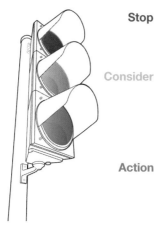

Stop Forgiveness is the cancelling of a debt in order that we ourselves can walk free.

Consider *'All the prophets testify about him that everyone who believes in him receives forgiveness of sins through his name'* (Acts 10:43).

Action Remember that forgiveness is an act of the will. During this week, consider any past experiences which may be robbing you of your peace of mind. Make a list of any individuals that come to mind and then personalize the prayer opposite accordingly.

As part of the ongoing process towards spiritual maturity, we need to acknowledge our sinful behaviour, tell God we are sorry and thank him for his forgiveness

Daily prayer for Week 9

Dear Father

I recognize that I have been unconditionally and totally forgiven for all my sin past, present and future. I understand that at salvation you lifted me from the line of Adam into Christ, wiping my slate completely clean. I know that the way to live in freedom is to extend and receive forgiveness on a daily basis.

With this in mind, I choose to forgive .... *(name)* for .... *(the action)* and for making me feel .... *(how you felt)*. I release .... *(name)* to you and ask that you would set me free from the bondage of the past.

Amen

life as it
could be

Week 10
No More Guilt
and Shame

Everyone, at some time or another, has experienced the dreadful sickening feeling in the pit of the stomach that accompanies a personal awareness of guilt or the sense of embarrassment, humiliation or anger that can accompany a feeling of shame.

Unfortunately, from the moment Adam and Eve chose to disobey God and experienced spiritual death, people have been making self-serving choices and been cruel to one another. One of the consequences of this behaviour is guilt and shame.

Due to the debilitating effect that guilt and shame has on a life of peace and freedom, Satan, the deceiver, will try and keep us in bondage to our past pain and mistakes.

The miracle of the grace that Jesus secured for us by dying on the cross, is that our loving heavenly Father does not allow past, present or future bad choices to distract or dilute his 100 per cent love for us.

With this understanding, we are able to receive and give forgiveness for past choices and, through the renewing of our mind, learn to live again as free people.

At a practical level, this involves taking control of our thoughts and living in the light of what God thinks about us, rather than how we have learnt to think about ourselves.

When we do behave in a way that is inconsistent with our identity as sons and daughters of God, we need to turn to him and receive his forgiveness again, and not allow Satan an opportunity to accuse.

Key message

Read Romans 8:1

Because of Jesus' sacrifice on the cross,

there is now no condemnation for those who are in Christ Jesus.

As Christians we should understand that it is our inclination to sin that produces guilt, which in turn can lead to shame. The beauty of forgiveness through Jesus is that we no longer have to carry the burden of the past.

Although there is no condemnation in God's eyes, and we can live in freedom from the power of guilt and shame, we always need to remember, and take responsibility for, the consequences of our choices.

The beauty of forgiveness through Jesus is that we no longer have to carry the burden of the past

Understanding

1 Our true identity in Christ means that we are no longer sinners in God's eyes, but righteous people with an inherited default toward selfish thinking and behaviour.

2 Satan, the deceiver, tempts us towards self-centred thoughts and actions because they lead us into guilt and shame and, if left unresolved, can cause us to move away from intimacy with the Lord.

3 It is fundamental for believers to understand how God sees us in relationship with him – with unconditional acceptance. (See the response of the father in the story of the lost son – Luke 15:11–32.)

4 With understanding of this truth, our relationship with God can mature into one where we experience his unconditional acceptance, rather than expecting acceptance based on our performance.

5 When we act in a way that is inconsistent with who we are in Christ, it is because our focus has shifted from operating in partnership with the Holy Spirit to doing things in our own strength.

6 Exercising the spiritual gift of 'self-control' is integral to eliminating the experience of guilt and shame.

Personal application

- During the course of this week, consider whether there is anything from your past that is still tying you up in guilt or shame. If the answer is yes, try to find someone (personal or professional) who could help you process your past.

- Other people can use guilt as a manipulative tool to make us do what they want us to do. Are you free enough to say 'No!' without feeling guilty?

- When Adam and Eve ate from the tree of knowledge they experienced guilt and shame, which caused them to hide from God. This is a natural human response. In light of the truth that there is no condemnation for those in Christ, do you feel able to turn to God rather than hide from him?

- Many well-known characters in the Bible made huge errors of judgement which resulted in personal guilt and shame. However, what set them apart was their ability to ask for and receive forgiveness, setting them free to pursue God's will for their life. Why not read about one of the following: Moses (in the books of *Exodus, Leviticus, Numbers, Deuteronomy*), David (in the books of *1* and *2 Samuel*), Peter (in the books of *Matthew, Mark, Luke, John* and *Acts*) or Paul (*Acts*).

- Are you at a place of freedom in your relationship with God, where you know your past has been dealt with and you now approach the future knowing that *'Everything is permissible . . . but not everything is beneficial'* (1 Corinthians 6:12)?

Christianity made simple

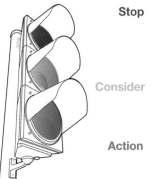

Stop   **Guilt and shame started with Adam and Eve in the garden and concluded for us, through Jesus, at the cross.**

Consider   *'There is now no condemnation for those who are in Christ Jesus'* (Romans 8:1).

Action   **At the beginning of each day this week, meditate and personalize Romans 8:1. *'There is now no condemnation* [for me, because I am] *in Christ Jesus.'***

Daily prayer for Week 10

Dear Father

I recognize that I have a past in which I have felt rejection and have rejected others. I have believed lies about myself and acted selfishly towards others. Out of self-interest, I have said and done things which have caused others pain and led to guilt and shame for myself.

As I walk with you towards spiritual maturity, I take hold of the truth that you do not condemn me. I leave the past behind and openly embrace your will for my future.

Amen

life as it
could be

Week 11
Acceptance

Most human relationships (even the closest ones) contain an expectation of 'acceptable' behaviour or performance. We learn in childhood what behaviour is good (acceptable) or bad (unacceptable). At school we also learn that if we do not behave properly we will get into trouble, or be rejected.

These lessons form the basis of our understanding of how to be good citizens and get by with our fellow man. However, when we carry the same principle into our relationship with God, it does not correlate in the same way. This is because our acceptability to God is not on the basis of either our behaviour or our performance, but on the basis of his grace to us.

It remains true that God does not sanction or approve of behaviour which is inconsistent with his nature; however, because Jesus atoned for our sins on the cross, God's love for us and acceptance of us is not diluted or affected by our behaviour.

Therefore, the good news for all believers is that even when we behave in a way that we regret and we know to be inconsistent with who we are as sons and daughters of God, we do not have to hide from him or fear his disapproval. Instead we can go straight to him to ask for forgiveness and restore intimacy, knowing that we are always acceptable in his eyes.

God's love for us and acceptance of us is not diluted or affected by our behaviour

Key message

Read Romans 8:38–39

For I am convinced that neither death nor life, neither angels nor demons, neither the present nor the future, nor any powers, neither height nor depth, nor anything else in all creation, will be able to separate us from the love of God that is in Christ Jesus our Lord.

Nothing can separate us from the love of God.

We are *always* acceptable to God, regardless of performance. The misconception many people have is that they move in and out of God's favour, based on their life choices. This process of constantly trying to please and appease can lead to emotional fatigue and result in disillusionment.

The truth, however, is that Jesus' sacrifice on the cross enables those of us who choose to receive his gift of grace to move from being 'unacceptable' in God's presence to 'acceptable' in God's presence – on the basis of what *he* has done, not what we can do. Remember, our acceptance is an issue related to our identity rather than behaviour. We are either 'in Adam' or born again 'in Christ'. There is no middle ground.

There is no such thing as a 'good Christian' or a 'bad Christian'; you are either a Christian or you are not a Christian. Thereafter it is a question of maturity.

Understanding

1 We are unacceptable to God when we are tainted with the inherited sin we received at birth. This is because God cannot have anything to do with sin.

2 On the cross, Jesus took our *unacceptability* upon himself and exchanged his *acceptability* for our inherited sin. Simply put, Christians swap sin and unacceptability for righteousness and acceptability. That's why it's called 'good news'!

3 With an understanding of our acceptability to God, we are able to enter into a relationship of freedom with him.

4 One of the enemy's main deceptions is to relentlessly attempt to convince us of the lie that we are failures and unacceptable, when the truth is that we are holy and righteous in the eyes of God, but our behaviour and desires are in the process of transformation.

5 Without an understanding of our acceptability to God, we can see him as a strict disciplinarian rather than a loving Father. Remember, the desire of his heart is always for our very best.

6 The outworking of this truth about our acceptance is that it provides us with the security and assurance to live life free from judgement and fear.

Personal application

- At the start of each day this week, thank God that whatever may occur and however you respond, you are totally and unconditionally acceptable to him.

- This week, as situations arise where you find yourself behaving in a way that is inconsistent with the nature of God, turn instantly to him and use it as an opportunity for personal development and spiritual maturing.

- The gospel message is truly liberating and sets us free from trying to achieve perfection. With this in mind, do you feel confident in your friendship with God?

- Given that we are unconditionally accepted by God and that we are his representatives here on earth, are we as accepting of others as he is of us?

- With your understanding of the subject of acceptance, do you think it is possible to be a 'backslidden' believer?

Do you feel confident in
your friendship with God?

Christianity made simple

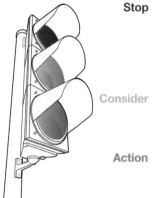

Stop   **Our unconditional acceptability, bought through Jesus' sacrifice, enables us to enter freely into relationship with God.**

Consider   **Nothing can separate us from the love of God (Romans 8:38–39).**

Action   **Think of a happy wedding scene from a film, book or real-life situation and take a snapshot in your mind of the love, joy and acceptance of that moment. Now consider the fact that God feels this way about you, regardless of your behaviour, at all times.**

Daily prayer for Week 11

Dear Father

I recognize that life has taught me that my 'lovability' is based upon my behaviour, and my natural tendency is to carry this understanding into my relationship with you.

Thank you that your acceptance of me is based on who you are and not on what I do. Help me to allow this truth to form the foundation of my relationship with you. May the outworking of this be my better understanding and acceptance of others.

Amen

life as it
could be

Week 12
Self or Christ?

The transition from dependency on *self* and our personal resources, to looking to *Jesus* to be our source of strength, guidance and sustenance does not happen overnight!

Because our self-life is all we have ever known, since it is our learnt natural way of being, it can take a while to be able to know, experientially, the difference between living out of our self-life and drawing on Christ's life through the Holy Spirit.

As discussed in previous chapters, God knows the limitations of our self-life and desires us to live life according to his original design.

Once we realize how inadequate, and indeed fatally flawed, our traditional methods of coping are (often resulting in exhaustion, anxiety or depression) we can make significant progress in the transition from self to Christ. We discover that through Jesus' presence there is a new way of living, which we would never have discovered if our self-life was still working for us. From this point, we experience a new way of being that, over time, proves to be far more satisfying than our old way of living.

This helps us to better understand what the apostle Paul is talking about when he says in 2 Corinthians 12:9 '*But he* [God] *said to me, "My grace is sufficient for you, for my power is made perfect in weakness."*'

When we find ourselves struggling to live in peace and freedom, it is often because our focus is not on Christ and his power and sufficiency but on ourselves.

Key message

Read Ephesians 2:3–5

All of us also lived among them at one time, gratifying the cravings of our sinful nature and following its desires and thoughts. Like the rest, we were by nature objects of wrath. But because of his great love for us, God, who is rich in mercy, made us alive with Christ even when we were dead in transgressions – it is by grace you have been saved.

As a consequence of the fall of mankind (Genesis 3) our inherited state of being is to live life independently of God (self-life). However, at the point of spiritual rebirth we are reconnected to God through Jesus Christ and given the resources to live life as God originally intended – dependent upon him.

Despite having all the resources of Christ available to us, the default mechanism for believers is always toward our self-life and independence, and it takes a conscious decision of the will to choose Christ over self.

It takes a conscious decision of the will to choose Christ over self

Understanding

1 The decision to choose Christ above self does not mean eradicating our individual uniqueness or personality but rather realigning ourselves to the blueprint of who God originally created us to be.

2 Before being reunited with God through salvation we only have our self-life to rely on (it's all we know). However, at the point of spiritual rebirth the 'treasure' and resource of Christ's sufficiency is deposited in us. *'But we have this treasure in jars of clay to show that this all-surpassing power is from God and not from us. We are hard pressed on every side, but not crushed; perplexed, but not in despair; persecuted, but not abandoned; struck down, but not destroyed. We always carry around in our body the death of Jesus, so that the life of Jesus may also be revealed in our body'* (2 Corinthians 4:7–10).

3 Our self-life means that unknowingly we develop a 'false self' derived from the coping mechanisms we have relied upon in order to live life independently of God. Once we become a Christian, this false self is in direct conflict with Christ's life in us and it takes time to both recognize what our false self looks like and, in turn, to learn to choose God's provision rather than our old ways.

4 Over time, as we choose Christ's life over our self-life, our 'true self' will emerge and we will begin to see ourselves as God intended – in fact, as he already sees us. Ultimately this transformation leads to a healthy self-worth (peace) based on who we are, not on what we do.

Personal application

- If we do not draw on Christ for life we always revert to self. Jesus took time away from people in order to spend time with God. Do you prioritize time with the Lord in the same way?

- Our fears drive many of the actions that form our self-life. This week think about your own life choices and consider how many of them are motivated by fear or selfishness?

- Satan's priority is to distract us from intimacy with God through the deception of believing that we are better off controlling life through our own self-effort, rather than relying on God. Does he tend to be an afterthought in your daily life?

- Over the next few days, stop and consider your own behavioural patterns and coping mechanisms. What tactics have you used in living life independently from God?

- At this point in your relationship with God, is your faith at a level where you believe his provision for your life is better than your own?

- Self-life is hard work and ultimately leads to soul fatigue; Christ's life leads to peace, contentment and freedom. Most of us continue in our own strength until life ceases to be manageable in one area or another. Is this your experience?

Christianity made simple

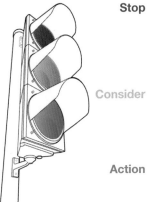

Stop Self-life = life independent from God

Christ's life = life in union with God

Consider *'But he said to me, "My grace is sufficient for you, for my power is made perfect in weakness"'* (2 Corinthians 12:9).

Action Begin the process of replacing self with Christ by considering a couple of your most obvious life-coping mechanisms. Pray the prayer overleaf with an expectation that the Lord will lead you away from self and into him.

What tactics have you used in living life independently from God?

Daily prayer for Week 12

Dear Father

I understand that when Adam and Eve ate from the fruit of the tree of knowledge, spiritual death occurred and we became self-sufficient.

I recognize that in my own life, the way I have learnt to cope is by .... and ....

I am learning that all of my needs can be met in you and that my self-life is a pale imitation of the richness of life that can be found in you. Help me to walk away from the familiarity of self and into an experience of abundant living.

Amen

life as it
could be

Week 13
Surrender

To be surrendered to God is to be able to say 'Yes, Lord,' to what ever he asks of you, and to be able to trust in his provision, whatever form that may take, at all times.

A surrendered heart, will and mind is able to trust in God's ability to work things out, while at the same time relinquishing control, when our natural human inclination is to manipulate, force our own agenda, or control a situation.

The Bible is full of examples of men and women who were surrendered to God. Abraham left his home in obedience to God, even though he did not know where he was going (Genesis 12; Hebrews 11:8); Moses went to Pharaoh to ask him to let the Israelites leave Egypt (Exodus 4 – 5); at great personal risk, Esther presented herself to the king (Esther 5); Simon Peter went back out to fish, even though he had been fishing all night, just because Jesus asked him to (Luke 5:5); and the ultimate surrender was by Jesus to the Father in the Garden of Gethsemane (Luke 22:42).

It is when we do live life surrendered to God that we experience the peace, freedom and power that we have been trying to gain by doing things in our own strength.

A surrendered heart, will and mind is able to trust in God's ability to work things out

Key message

Read Philippians 3:7–9

But whatever was to my profit I now consider loss for the sake of Christ. What is more, I consider everything a loss compared to the surpassing greatness of knowing Christ Jesus my Lord, for whose sake I have lost all things. I consider them rubbish, that I may gain Christ and be found in him, not having a righteousness of my own that comes from the law, but that which is through faith in Christ – the righteousness that comes from God and is by faith.

The word 'surrender' is used to describe the deliberate choice to give to God every aspect of our lives and relinquish control to him on a daily and moment by moment basis.

As believers we are often reluctant to surrender the things we cling to for identity and security. It is these very things that the apostle Paul is talking about in the passage above which he gladly surrenders, knowing that only Christ leads to peace and freedom.

$$\frac{\text{Identity \& security}}{\text{Fear of loss}} \quad = \quad \text{Anxiety and stress}$$

Understanding

1 Our natural response to surrender is to look at what we will lose rather than what we will gain. Because we are so geared towards self-survival we probably associate surrender with weakness and then out of fear of loss we hang on to the very things which keep us in bondage.

2 An unwillingness to surrender has in its foundation a lack of trust that God's provision will far exceed anything we are able to provide for ourselves. This leads to a conflict between our self-life and our life in the Spirit, which can result in anxiety, control, manipulative behaviour, stress, depression and sometimes complete personal 'meltdown'.

3 From a place of relinquishing control we can experience the love and grace of God in a totally new and wonderful way. Our unwillingness to surrender the things we cling on to prevents us from experiencing the truth of God's love.

4 One of Satan's favourite tricks is to have us believe that the things we fear losing are fundamental for living life well. The truth, however, is that our well-being is found in Christ, with all other things added on, in accordance with God's will. Jesus knew this when he said, *'But seek first his kingdom and his righteousness, and all these things will be given to you as well'* (Matthew 6:33).

5 Surrender is all about entrusting the things and people that we hold dear to the God of love, whose desire is for our very best.

Personal application

- This week make a list in priority order of the things that you hold on to and find hard to surrender to God. Can you identify the underlying fear associated with each area?

- As you interact with the world this week, consider the main temptations and fears that Satan uses to distract people from being surrendered to God?

- Are you surrendered to God in the area of your personal wealth? Do you consider yourself a 'steward' or the 'owner' of your earthly possessions?

- Over the next few days, consider the possibility that money can feed independence (self-life) rather than dependency on God. Is your identity in God and his provision or your work and your possessions?

- Time and again the Bible reveals to us people of faith who were surrendered to God and received tremendous blessing. Do you truly believe that God's way is always best?

Do you truly believe that God's way is always best?

Christianity made simple

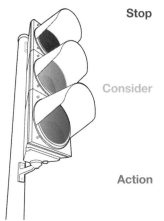

Stop Surrender does not mean giving up everything you value; it means holding everything before the Lord in open hands.

Consider *'Simon answered, "Master, we've worked hard all night and haven't caught anything. But because you say so, I will let down the nets"'* (Luke 5:5).

Action At the beginning of each day this week, pray the prayer opposite, specifically surrendering the areas or fears identified in the first point in the Application section.

Our unwillingness to surrender the things we cling on to prevents us from experiencing the truth of God's love

Daily prayer for Week 13

Dear Father

During the course of my life I have collected or clung on to
.... and have grown to fear losing them. This fear
produces anxiety and stress.

Today I step out in faith and surrender these things and people to
you. Your word challenges me to believe that your perfect love can
replace my fears.

Please remove any fear in my heart and replace it with your peace
and freedom.

Amen

life as it could be

Week 14

Meltdown

None of us like it when we find that we are unable to cope in an area of life, or experience the devastation of seeing our hopes, dreams or all that we have been working towards come crashing down around us.

For a believer, such experiences of personal 'meltdown' can lead to a crisis of faith: 'Why has God allowed these things to happen to me?' During these times, a healthy understanding of our lives and the world around us viewed from a heavenly perspective can be really helpful.

Our self-life and independent behaviour is actually a barrier to us receiving and enjoying peace in life through Christ. None of us would choose to experience personal difficulties. However, from a position of desiring the very best for us, God will sometimes allow us to experience difficulty and disillusionment so that we may go on to experience even greater freedom in him. When we come to the end of ourselves it is often referred to as 'brokenness' by Christians.

Ironically, the Bible says that we should view personal crises as a blessing – although it certainly doesn't feel like it at the time! God has much to teach us through these times and so the question to be asked is not, 'Why is this happening to me?' but rather, 'Father, what are you teaching me and showing me at this time?'

The Bible gives us many examples of very capable individuals who God allowed to experience the destruction of their self-life and pride in order to reshape their character and focus. Joseph, through betrayal and imprisonment; Moses, through the repercussions of murdering an Egyptian; Job, in losing all that he held dear; Peter, in his denial of Christ; and Paul, on the road to Damascus.

Key message

Read James 1:2–4

Consider it pure joy, my brothers, whenever you face trials of many kinds, because you know that the testing of your faith develops perseverance. Perseverance must finish its work so that you may be mature and complete, not lacking anything.

God is not only concerned about our salvation, he also wants us to know freedom from our self-life and the fears, abuses and experiences that keep human beings captive.

Meltdown occurs when a person's own coping mechanisms and self-life are shown to be insufficient for life's challenges and demands. In these incredibly difficult times, God encourages us to confront the pain or fear and draw on his strength to begin a process of healing, leading to freedom. This is the time when faith truly moves from theory into practice.

Meltdown occurs when a person's own coping mechanisms and self-life are shown to be insufficient for life's challenges and demands

Understanding

1 If we choose to live our life independently from God we will miss out on the freedom of life that God intended for us. If we try to live our life in our own strength we will at some point come to the end of our own resources resulting in personal meltdown, causing us to reflect on the limitations of self.

2 In order to live in Christ, we need to believe that relying on him is better than trying to cope in our own strength. Most of us do not come to this place of faith naturally, but through extreme circumstances we can find ourselves reaching beyond our own resources, out to God.

3 During times of emotional or physical breakdown, our tendency is to try to get back to familiar forms of coping (self-sufficiency) rather than establish a foundation for a completely different way of living. We need to learn to allow the Holy Spirit to become the leading force in our life, with our body and soul in submission, rather than the other way around.

4 Living our life in Christ will not exclude us from difficult times, but in those times we will have the Spirit of Christ and his resources to draw on. He will give us a totally different perspective on our problems and the strength to get through them victoriously. *'No, in all these things we are more than conquerors through him who loved us'* (Romans 8:37).

5 In the midst of challenging times it is important to remember that God's desire is always for our very best. *'And we know that in all things God works for the good of those who love him, who have been called according to his purpose'* (Romans 8:28). When experiencing a time of turmoil, remember to ask God for faith and his perspective.

95

Personal application

- During this week, think back over your life's history and consider the events, circumstances and people leading up to difficult periods. Are there any consistent themes or situations that have led to your pain?

- Consider whether any of these situations reveal a habitual pattern of behaviour driven by an instinct to get your identity and desires met by relying on your own resources rather than God.

- In order to break the cycle of circumstances which continue to keep you from experiencing freedom, consider whether you are holding something against someone – whether you need to forgive yourself, another person or even God.

- During this week, read the story of Joseph in Genesis, chapters 37 to 50, and imagine how you would have felt in his situation? Do you see how God shaped his character through painful experiences?

Are there any consistent themes or situations that have led to your pain?

Christianity made simple

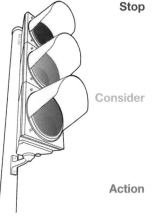

Stop When we come to an understanding of the limitations of self, we are on the verge of experiencing life as it could be.

Consider *'I am the vine; you are the branches. If a man remains in me and I in him, he will bear much fruit; apart from me you can do nothing'* (John 15:5).

Action Remember, in times of struggle, instead of saying 'Why is this happening to me?' ask 'Father, what do you want to teach me?'

Daily prayer for Week 14

Dear Father

I recognize that living life in my own strength, rather than depending on you, has led me to times of personal meltdown.

The Bible shows me that all men and women of faith go through a process of learning to rely on you and believe, in faith, that your ways are always better than ours.

What I really desire is to live according to your plans and purposes. Please illuminate and heal any areas of my life that are in conflict with your will.

Amen

life as it
could be

Week 15
**Suffering and
Sorrow**

To experience suffering and sorrow is a part of being human. We live in a fallen and imperfect world full of fallen and imperfect people, and at some point we all have to deal with pain, hardship, abuse or bereavement.

When we experience suffering and sorrow, we quite understandably ask God to take away our pain (as the Bible encourages us to), but if God decides not to act in the way we would like him to or with the speed we are looking for, it can leave us feeling despondent, confused or unheard.

Our perception that our prayers are not being answered can leave us thinking that God does not care. Some Christian teaching even suggests that the reason we are not experiencing 'breakthrough' is down to our lack of faith. Whilst that kind of formula might appear to absolve God, it leaves us not only in pain but also feeling inadequate.

As we saw in the previous chapter, the apostle Paul reminds us that *'in all things God works for the good of those who love him'* (Romans 8:28), and that includes the times we are struggling. In many ways we learn the most and grow in faith the most during times of hardship. In God's eyes, times of suffering and sorrow are not times of punishment but an opportunity to deepen our faith and discover that he will meet all our needs, instead of relying on ourselves.

Our perception that our prayers are not being answered can leave us thinking that God does not care

Key message

Read Luke 22:39–44

'Father, if you are willing, take this cup from me; yet not my will, but yours be done' (v.42).

Many people find it hard to reconcile suffering and sorrow with a loving God. Jesus, however, never allowed his personal fear of suffering and sorrow to dissuade him from fulfilling God's plan and purpose for his life.

In the context of spiritual realignment we begin to understand that suffering and sorrow can lead to brokenness and the dismantling of our self-life, causing us to be open to God in a way that we would not be naturally inclined to. Suffering and sorrow are a direct consequence of the Fall and in our fallen human state we quite naturally want to avoid experiencing either. However, once we understand that God is 100 per cent for us, we see suffering not as God punishing us but as an opportunity to depend upon his ability to sustain us, rather than relying on ourselves.

Jesus never allowed his personal fear of suffering and sorrow to dissuade him from fulfilling God's plan

Understanding

1 In order to truly understand suffering and sorrow we need to go back to the Garden of Eden and ask the question, 'Why did God curse Adam and Eve after they had eaten from the tree of the knowledge of good and evil?' Could it be that our loving Father actually understood that once they had achieved independence (self-life), the only way to bring them back to him was through a process of allowing them to experience how deficient their self-life was?

2 No one of sound mind desires suffering and sorrow. Most of us experience it as a consequence of either coming to the end of ourselves (like the lost son in Luke 15:11–32) or as a result of living in a fallen world. However, as we grow in spiritual maturity and faith it is possible to endure life's tribulations, disappointments and losses with the perspective that *in all circumstances* God is working for the good of those who love him (Romans 8:28).

3 It is important to recognize that it was not God's design for humanity to experience pain. As individuals we are born into a fallen world where suffering and sorrow form part of our daily lives. Jesus (through his death on the cross) has already accomplished reconciliation for us with the Father. However, until we are united with him in heaven, hardship will be part of our lives.

Personal application

- Read 2 Corinthians 12:7–10. It is clear from this passage that Paul suffered in some way and that God allowed it to continue. However, like Jesus, Paul accepted that this formed part of his spiritual journey and surrendered to God's greater wisdom. Is your faith such that you can trust God to this extent?

- Looking at the example set by Jesus and Paul in regard to surrender, what characteristics or disciplines do you think enabled them to face the suffering they were called to endure (see 2 Corinthians 11:23–33)?

- Episodes of suffering and sorrow provide an opportunity for reflection and reassessment, which can result in us either moving away from God or drawing closer to him. This week, reflect on your own past and your reaction to hardships. Do you believe that you are able to maintain a positive relationship with God regardless of your circumstances?

- Given that *'in all things God works for the good of those who love him'* (Romans 8:28), have you ever experienced a situation of short-term pain which has resulted in long-term benefit? If so, how has this shaped your faith?

- Do you understand that suffering in the world occurs as a direct result of the Fall, not as a punishment from a distant God, and that we can look forward to a time when creation will be re-established in perfection? (Read Revelation 21:1–5.)

Christianity made simple

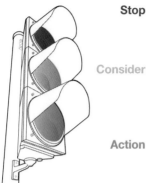

Stop   **Even in the midst of suffering and sorrow God has your best interests at heart.**

Consider   *'He was despised and rejected by men, a man of sorrows, and familiar with suffering'* (Isaiah 53:3).

Action   **Times of trouble can either be times when we allow doubt to enter our hearts or can be opportunities to discover greater intimacy with God. The choice is ours.**

Daily prayer for Week 15

Dear Father

I understand that you are love and that you desire the very best for me. I recognize that suffering and sorrow are part of this fallen world and originate from Satan, the enemy of God and man. You are the Creator of all that is good and are able to bring light out of even the darkest circumstances.

Help me to trust you and deepen my experience of you whatever tomorrow brings.

May your will be done.

Amen

life as it
could be

Week 16

Security and
Intimacy with God

According to the Bible, when God first created the world, everything was perfect. God provided for mankind's every need and Adam and Eve had no reason not to fully trust in their God. Life in the Garden of Eden provided security and intimacy of relationship.

After their decision to disobey God, sin affected mankind's ability to trust both God and his fellow man. Security and intimacy had been breached by betrayal.

Jesus' atoning death on the cross has not only paid the price for the sin that separated us from God, it has also given us back the opportunity for security and intimacy with God. However, because we have all experienced something of the harshness of living with less than perfect people, in a less than perfect world, we have learnt to be sceptical about trusting others, and especially someone we cannot see!

God encourages us to rediscover relational intimacy with him through the Holy Spirit and to look to him as the one to meet our needs.

Everything that once stood in the way of our intended love relationship with our Creator has now been removed; all we need now is the faith to believe it!

Sin affected mankind's ability to trust both God and his fellow man

Key message

Read Ephesians 2:8–10

For it is by grace that you have been saved, through faith – and this is not from yourselves, it is the gift of God – not by works so that no one can boast. For we are God's workmanship, created in Christ Jesus to do good works, which God prepared in advance for us to do.

If through reading this book you have experienced a greater revelation of why the 'Good News' really is good news, then you have begun the journey towards experiencing greater intimacy with God.

Relational intimacy with God is only possible when laid upon a foundation of the truth that we are saved by grace, not by works, and have been lifted from the family of Adam into the family of Christ.

This gift frees us from condemnation and performance-based religious behaviour, enabling us to pursue intimacy with God, secure in the knowledge that Christ has paid the debt for our sin once and for all.

As we pursue spiritual maturity from this position of security, knowing God's love and acceptance, we are freed from our self-life and all that goes with it, enabling us to draw our self-worth and identity from intimate relationship with God.

Understanding

1 The most important thing for a believer to know in terms of security is that, once we are reconciled to God through Christ, our future is sealed and secure. What we do from then on does not affect our salvation. However, the apostle Paul, writing to the Corinthians says, *'Everything is permissible – but not everything is beneficial'* (1 Corinthians 10:23) i.e. although our salvation is complete, our personal choices will affect the level of intimacy we experience in our relationship with God.

2 With an understanding of this security, we can begin to operate out of a desire to do God's will, knowing that his way really is best for us, rather than continuing to make choices driven by our self-life or a fear of what God or others may think of us.

3 Jesus understood that intimacy with the Father was the most important thing, closely followed by love for others (Matthew 22:37–40). The apostle Paul continued this theme in Philippians 2:1–11, where he taught that acts of service are an overflow of our intimate relationship with God, rather than an attempt to repay a debt.

4 All intimate human relationships are born out of trust and a feeling of security with another individual. The same dynamic is also true of our relationship with God.

Once we are reconciled to God through Christ, our future is sealed and secure

Personal application

- Over the course of this week, and the weeks to come, establish once and for all in your mind and in your heart that when you are reunited with God through Christ, relationally, from the Lord's point of view, everything is always OK.

- Do you struggle to have a close relationship with God? If you find this difficult, consider whether it could be for one of the following reasons: personal shame, a lack of understanding, a habitual problem, fear, indifference, distractions, a lack of faith. If you are able to identify any of these areas, talk to God about it and ask for his insight as to the way forward.

- A good indicator for the nature of your relationship with the Lord is your 'thought talk'. Is it full of 'I must', 'I should', 'I ought', 'I have to', etc.? Or is it more consistent with how you would relate to a close friend or loved one?

- What would you consider the fundamental driving force of your relationship with the Lord to be – love or fear?

- Paul wrote in Romans 8:28–39 that *nothing* can separate a believer from the love of God. Think about whether the foundation of your relationship with the Lord is built on this truth.

Do you struggle to have a close relationship with God?

Christianity made simple

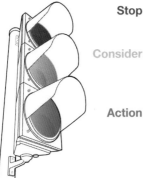

Stop   **Nothing can separate you from the love of God!**

Consider   *'You are forgiving and good, O Lord, abounding in love to all who call to you'* (Psalm 86:5).

Action   **Walk in the security of God's unwavering commitment to you. You are free to enjoy intimate relationship with him on a daily basis.**

Daily prayer for Week 16

Dear Father

As I continue on my journey with you, thank you for the fact that I now know you are love and that, no matter how often I mess things up, you are *always* there to forgive, heal and encourage me onwards.

As I walk with you into the future, help me to get to know you better, that I might feel totally secure in surrendering to you, that I might know more of your peace, and that your values would be lived out in my life.

Amen

Glossary of Terms

Adam and Eve The first man and woman to be created.

(In) Adam Meaning that we are all descendants of Adam and as such unfortunately inherit his fallen state as a result of his disobedience in the Garden of Eden . . . it's in our spiritual DNA.

Bible versions
NASB New American Standard Bible. One of the most literally translated of the English language Bible versions.
NIV New International Version. One of the most popular and widely read modern versions.
The Message A contemporary language version by Eugene H. Peterson, written in a style aimed at facilitating easy and enjoyable reading.

Body, soul and spirit
Body Comprising our physical being including our five senses
Soul Our mind, emotions and will (our personality)
Spirit Our true identity from which we communicate with God

Born again The term used to express the process of someone's spirit coming alive to God.

Brokenness or meltdown When we come to an understanding or experience of the insufficiency of our own ability to cope with life.

(In) Christ We can continue to live out of our own resources (self-life) or look to live life as God originally intended by learning to live according to his will, out of daily experience and relationship with him.

Christian The name given to those who have accepted Jesus Christ as their Lord and Saviour.

Faith Believing and trusting in God more than you believe in yourself. The ability to trust what we cannot see – Hebrews 11:1.

The Fall The term used to describe the result of Adam and Eve's decision to disobey God's instructions which resulted in their spiritual separation from him.

Flesh (self-life) Also referred to as *'sinful nature'* in the NIV. This term is used by Paul in his New Testament letters to describe how we choose to cope with life outside of a relationship with God.

Garden of Eden The place where Adam and Eve lived prior to the Fall.

Kingdom of Heaven The arena in which God's values and life rule, both in heaven and here on earth.

Paul, the Apostle The man known as Saul the Pharisee before meeting with Jesus on the road to Damascus and becoming the man who established many of the early churches. Paul is the author of many of the books in the New Testament which are his letters of instruction to those churches.

Prayer Communication with God, whether in solitude, a group setting or general day-to-day conversation. (We would encourage you to think of prayer as something you do in everything you do!)

Righteousness To be perfect in God's sight.

Satan Also referred to as **'the Enemy'** or **'the Devil'** who is committed to preventing people from experiencing the love of God.

Sin The expression used to describe the condition of mankind in his/her natural unsaved state which was the result of Adam and

Eve's rebellion against God. Sin forms the barrier between God and man which is the product of the Fall.

Sins Actions, thoughts, etc. that are contrary to God's will and purpose.

Sin, indwelling The product of the Fall; the bias towards self-orientated behaviour that exists in each of us.

Spiritual growth/spiritual maturity The lifetime pursuit of surrendering our self-life and replacing our independence with dependency on God.

Surrender The act of voluntarily submitting to the will of God.

The world An expression used in the Bible to denote the arena in which mankind lives and the influence that this unredeemed world has on humanity when decisions are based on self rather than on relationship with God.